CHRISTINE AND SYLVIE HOOGHE

CRYSTAL
BEADED JEWELLERY

Rings, necklaces and other sparkling jewels

PHOTOGRAPHS: CLAIR CURT

Search Press

CONTENTS

Materials

Beads

Swarovski crystal beads

These beads are machine cut, using a very precise method perfected by the company. They catch the light and give jewellery a brilliant sparkle.

They come in a variety of shapes and an extensive range of colours. The jewellery in this book is created mainly from bicone beads (4 mm, 5 mm, 6 mm, and 8 mm) and teardrops. Details are given at the start of each piece of jewellery.

Seed beads (also known as rocailles)

Seed beads are small, round, glass beads. They come in several different sizes. The most commonly used are about 2.5 mm in diameter. The smallest, which mix very well with the crystal bicones, are 2 mm in diameter. There are also tubular beads of different lengths and diameters. To make sure your jewels are consistent, always choose beads that have been carefully graded.

Faceted beads

Made of translucent or opaque coloured glass, usually moulded, faceted beads go well with crystal beads, setting them off and counterbalancing their angularity.

faceted beads

bicone beads

small seed beads

Other beads

Small glass beads, oval (or rice) beads or cultured pearls go perfectly with crystal. Vary the shapes and effects! On the other hand, large plastic beads, flashy metal beads and ethnic beads are not recommended.

teardrop beads

medium seed beads

One colour at a time or in bold combinations, crystals can be put together in many different ways. Try the mixtures out by putting a few beads in a pot of a neutral colour or in the palm of your hand. To give you a better idea, add the other beads you wish to use.

tubular beads

other beads

Threads

Nylon thread

Flexible, slightly stretchy and transparent, nylon thread is suitable for most projects using crystal beads. Use a thread of gauge 0.35mm or 0.25mm, depending on the number of times the thread will pass through the beads. Always pull the nylon thread evenly and very gently, in order to avoid cutting it by rubbing against the edges of crystal beads.

Flexible beading wire

Made of metal wires (silvery, golden or coloured) twisted together and coated with nylon, this thread is very firm and is generally reserved for simple strings of heavy or sharp-edged beads. It can add to the beauty of the piece, if allowed to remain partly visible in between lightweight beads (see p. 12).

Copper and brass wires

These are definitely not recommended for use with crystal beads, as they chip the edges when you pull them through. However, you may find them useful with other beads and for certain ways of finishing off. Check the list of materials given for each project.

Findings

This term describes all the small accessories that are needed for finishing off pieces of jewellery.

Clasps

The simplest models such as spring clasps or lobster-claw clasps are very suitable for crystal beads. Gold, silver or copper-coloured, matt or shiny... choose the finish that blends in best with your beads.

Crimp beads

These extremely useful, metal beads enable you to attach the clasps without knots, which look ugly in nylon thread and are impossible to do with beading wire. For instructions, see page 10.

Jump rings

Rings of various diameters are used to link the jewellery and join the different components.

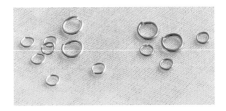

Metal wires

These are relatively flexible, can be cut, and are easy to bend with pliers. The ones with heads (head pins) can be used to make dangles. Joining wires (eye pins), which have no heads but have a loop at one end, can be used to make articulated jewels.

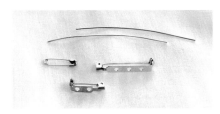

Brooch backs

These come in various lengths and are usually fixed to crystal bead jewels by discreet "sewing". A safety pin is fine for small brooches.

Earring wires

There are different models for pierced and non-pierced ears. You can attach beads directly to lever-back earring wires with shell motifs, also known as French clips (see p. 38).

Jewellery pliers

These are easily obtainable from all bead and craft shops. They are small and very easy to handle.

Wire cutters: used for cutting metal wires or thick beading wire.

Round nose pliers: used for making loops in pins or wires.

Flat nose pliers: used for holding small items, opening and closing rings, and squeezing crimp beads.

For finishing off, when a little precision is needed, do not hesitate to use the round nose and flat nose pliers at the same time, one in each hand.

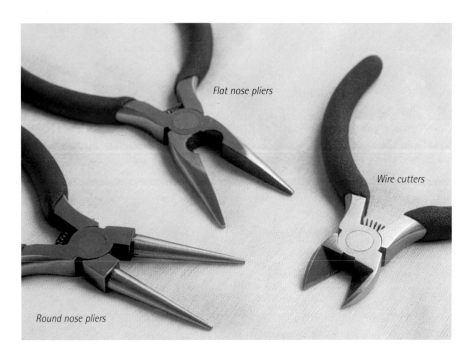

Flat nose pliers

Wire cutters

Round nose pliers

Use the flat nose pliers for crimp beads.

Beading needles

In specialist shops you can find long thin needles for threading beads. They are only suitable for the thinnest threads. Thick threads are stiffer, enabling you to work without a needle.

Crush the end of the nylon thread between your front teeth to make it easier to thread through the eye.

Needles are essential for making some pieces of jewellery and optional for others, so it is up to you to choose the solution you feel most comfortable with. Never force a needle through a bead, as you risk breaking it.

Glue

To strengthen certain ways of finishing off, use contact adhesive or transparent nail varnish.

Advice

Following the sketches

To make the sketches easier to follow, these illustrations are used in the book: to distinguish between two strands of a single thread, one is coloured red and the other blue.

To make some of the more complicated sketches easier to follow, beads that are threaded twice are emphasised by a darker outline.

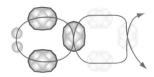

Start

The start is shown by an arrow. The beads strung in step 1 are shown in grey in the next step and only new stringings are shown.

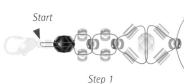

Start

Step 1

Step 2

Workspace

It is important to arrange your workspace well, especially when making the more elaborate pieces. Make sure it is well lit. Work on a tray and keep the boxes of beads and your current piece of work on it, so that if a box of beads is accidentally knocked over, the beads will not scatter.

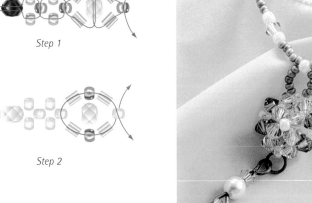

Levels of difficulty

The level of difficulty of each piece is indicated by the number of beads.

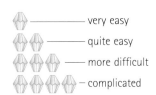

———— very easy

——— quite easy

—— more difficult

— complicated

Adaptable jewellery

Making your own jewellery offers several advantages, including being able to adapt it perfectly to the size you want. To guide you in your personal projects, these are the approximate lengths of the finished pieces (including finishing off and clasps).

Bracelet: 17 to 20 cm (7 to 8 ins), depending on the size of the wrist and the size of the beads used.
Choker: approximately 40 cm (16 ins).
Small necklace: 50 to 60 cm (20 to 24 ins).
Long chain: 80 cm to 3 m (32 ins to 10 ft), depending on how many times you want to wind it round.

Techniques

Finishing with a knot

This way of finishing off is used when you are not attaching a clasp.

Make 2 or 3 simple knots one on top of the other. If possible, thread one of the strands through one of the neighbouring beads and pull it, in order to hide the knot inside the bead. Then thread the strands through several beads before cutting them off.

If it is not possible to thread the strands through, cut them off after the knots and strengthen the knot with a spot of contact adhesive or transparent nail varnish.

Attaching a clasp using crimp beads

This method can be used on both nylon thread and flexible beading wire.

After the last bead, thread a crimp bead, then pass the thread through one of the two parts of the clasp. Thread it back the other way through the crimp bead and the next few beads. Ensure there is no room for movement between the beads. Squeeze the crimp bead with the flat nose pliers.

To make this way of finishing look prettier, you can put a bead of the same kind as the rest of the piece in between the clasp and the crimp bead.

Opening and closing a jump ring

It is easier to do this using two pairs of pliers. In order not to distort the ring, it is best to open it by twisting. Gently pull one end of the ring towards you and push the other one away from you. Use the same method to close it again.

Making a small chain

Small chains are very useful for adjusting the size of chokers and bracelets. Simply link a few jump rings together. You can create an interesting effect by alternating rings of two different sizes.

Dangles

Much more than a mere detail, a dangle attached to the clasp of a jewel gives it an extra touch of originality and makes it easier to fasten.

Thread the beads of your choice on to a head pin. Using wire cutters, cut the pin off about 1 cm (³/₈ in) above the last bead and form a ring using the round nose pliers.

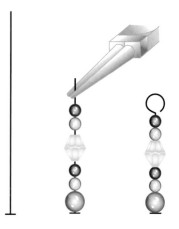

Dewdrops

Choker

Erinite   Sapphire   Peridot   Blue zircon

Sapphire   White opal   Olivine

Materials

◈ Choker

25 to 30 size 4, 5, 6, and 8 mm bicones in assorted colours

50 to 60 crimp beads

Lobster-claw clasp and ring

Green or gold-coloured flexible beading wire

Flat nose pliers

1 Cut about 60 cm (24 ins) wire. String the first bead in the middle of the wire and fix it by squeezing a crimp bead on each side of it.

Fix the other beads on either side of it, spacing them 0.5 to 1 cm ($^3/_{16}$ to $^3/_8$ in) apart. To make the necklace more unusual, avoid placing 2 beads of the same colour or size opposite one another.

2 Finish by attaching the clasp and the ring as shown in the sketch. Cut off the excess wire.

Crimp bead

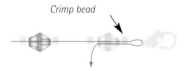

Earrings

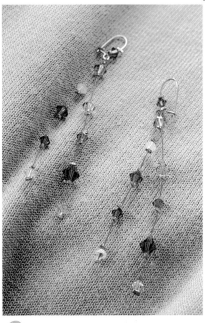

Materials

Earrings

Two lots of ten, size 4, 5 and 6 mm bicones in assorted colours

About 20 crimp beads

Simple gold-coloured earring wires

Green or gold-coloured flexible beading wire

Toothpick or yarn needle

Flat nose pliers

1 Slide a 4 mm bicone with a crimp bead on either side onto an earring wire (see photo). If necessary, force the earring wire open a little. Squeeze the crimp beads.

2 Double a 20 cm (8 in) length of wire round a tooth-pick. Thread a 5 mm bicone with a crimp bead on each side on both strands and push right up to the tooth-pick. Squeeze the crimp beads.

3 Fix the remaining beads onto each strand separately to make a dangle about 7 cm (3 ins) long. Cut off the excess wire after the last crimp bead. Slide the dangle onto the earring wire. Make a second earring to match.

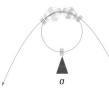

a

b

Rings

Materials

Rings

2 or 3 size 4 to 6 mm bicones in assorted colours

3 to 7 crimp beads

Green or gold-coloured flexible beading wire

Flat nose pliers

On a 25 cm (10 in) length of wire, string 2 or 3 bicones with crimp beads before and after (or on either side of each bead), plus one extra crimp bead. Thread one strand of the wire back through the beads of the motif and adjust the ring to fit your finger (a). Squeeze the crimp beads of the motif, taking care not to alter the size of the ring.

Cross the strands in the remaining crimp bead. Squeeze it, then cut off the excess wire (b).

Baroque Gold

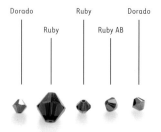

Dorado — Ruby — Ruby — Dorado — Ruby AB — Dorado

Bracelet

Materials

Bracelet

6 mm faceted beads: 5 iridescent dark red

4 mm faceted beads: 2 iridescent dark red, 5 gold-coloured

8 gold-coloured bicones (Dorado)

Iridescent red seed beads

Gold-coloured tubular beads

Small copper-coloured seed beads

Gold-coloured lobster-claw clasp and ring

Gold-coloured jump rings

Head pin

Nylon thread gauge 0.35 mm

2 crimp beads

Flat nose and round nose pliers

Beading needles (optional)

1. Using a crimp bead, fix the clasp in the middle of a thread 1.5 m (60 ins) long to give 2 identical strands. Thread them both together through a small, dark red faceted bead, then cross them in the next beads as shown in the sketch.

2. Thread one of the strands back through the beads around the centre bead and add 2 new red seed beads.

3. Continue by crossing the 2 strands in the next beads. Ease the bicones gently into place, to avoid cutting the thread.

4. Complete motif (a), then repeat it 3 more times. Work motif (b) one more time to finish the bracelet.

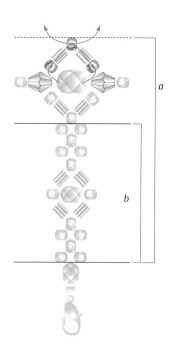

5. **Finishing.** Thread both strands through the second small, dark red faceted bead and attach a ring, using a crimp bead. Add a small chain, then a dangle mounted on a head pin (see p. 10).

Earrings

Materials

Earrings

Iridescent dark red faceted beads: 2
size 6 mm and 2 size 4 mm

2 size 4 mm gold-coloured faceted
beads

4 gold-coloured bicones (Dorado)

Gold-coloured short tubular beads

Iridescent red seed beads

Small copper-coloured seed beads

Gold-coloured French clips with shell
motif

2 head pins

2 fine gauge jump rings

Nylon thread gauge 0.25 mm

Flat nose and round nose pliers

Beading needles (optional)

*N.B. Check that the holes in the red seed
beads are big enough to take a ring plus
two strands of nylon thread.*

1 **Dangle.** Make a dangle on a head pin
with a small faceted bead and an iridescent red seed bead (see p. 10). Slide it to the
middle of a 30 cm (12 in) length of thread,
then string the first beads as in the sketch.

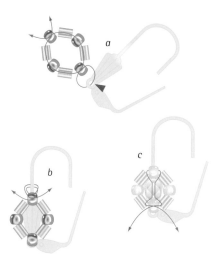

2 To finish the central motif, string gold tubular beads and red seed beads onto each strand, thread both strands back through the faceted bead, then add the second bicone.

3 String the last of the beads, crossing the strands as in the sketch. Slide a seed bead onto a jump ring and thread the strands through it. Knot the ends. Thread them back through a few beads.

4 **Decorating the earring wire.** Thread a 20 cm (8 in) length of thread through the hole in the earring wire, so the wire is in the middle of the thread. Cross the two ends through a red seed bead, then string the other seed beads as shown in sketch (a).

Attach the top of the assembly above the shell by threading both strands back through the last bead (b).

Then thread both strands together through the central bead and cross them in the first seed bead. Knot the ends behind the shell and feed them back through a few beads before cutting off. (c).

5 **Finishing.** Fix the dangle to the earring wire using the jump ring.

Materials

Faceted ring

Iridescent dark red faceted beads:
1 size 6 mm and 2 size 4 mm

Iridescent red seed beads

Gold-coloured short tubular beads

Small copper-coloured seed beads

Nylon thread gauge 0.35 mm

Bicone ring

Bicones: 1 size 8 mm deep pink (Ruby) and 2 size 4 mm deep pink (Ruby AB)

Iridescent red seed beads

Small copper-coloured seed beads

Nylon thread gauge 0.35 mm

Rings

The rings are made in the same way as the bracelet using 50 cm (20 ins) of thread.

1 **Faceted ring.** String the first seed bead in the middle of the thread to leave 2 strands of equal length. Start the ring and then make the central motif (a).

b

2 Once the central motif has been completed (sketches b, c, and d), finish the ring, adapting its length to your finger size.

c

3 Close the ring by threading one of the strands through the first bead again. Try the ring on before finally tying the knot. Feed the ends back through the beads before cutting them off.

d

knot

Bicone ring

Venice

Light smoked topaz

Light smoked topaz

Light peach

Chrysolite

Ring

Materials

◈ Ring

8 mm imitation cultured pearl

4 mm bicones: 2 Light peach, 2 Light smoked topaz, 2 Chrysolite

White pearlised seed beads, plus 2 in pale green

Small pearlised beige seed beads

Nylon thread gauge 0.25 mm

Beading needles (optional)

◈◈ Necklace

4 mm bicones: 15 Light peach, 12 Light smoked topaz, 14 Chrysolite

White pearlised seed beads

Small pearlised beige seed beads

8 mm pale pink faceted bead

5 mm imitation cultured pearl

Light smoked topaz crystal teardrop bead

Fine-gauge antiqued metal jump ring

Antiqued metal wire

2 crimp beads

Nylon thread gauge 0.25 mm and 0.35 mm

Flat nose pliers

Round nose pliers

Beading needles (recommended)

N.B. Check the holes in the white pearlised seed beads are big enough for a ring plus two strands of 0.25 mm nylon thread.

1 Cut 80 cm (32 ins) thread. String the first seed beads in the middle of the thread, then cross the strands through one of the green bicones. Begin the central motif as shown in the sketch.

2 Thread one of the strands through the beads around the central pearl and add 2 green seed beads. String 1 white seed bead on each strand. Make the ring the desired length by stringing groups of 3 beige seed beads on each strand alternately and crossing the strands in a white seed bead.

3 Close the ring by threading one of the strands through the first bead again. Try it on before tying the final knot. Feed the ends through a few beads before cutting off.

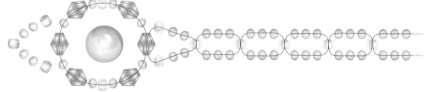

Necklace

Flower ball

1 Slip 1 white seed bead onto the jump ring and close it. Cut 50 cm (20 ins) of 0.25 mm thread. String 1 white seed bead in the middle. Then string the bicones for the flowers on the top, front and back faces of the ball, crossing the strands in the seed beads, including the one attached to the jump ring. Cross strands in the first seed bead to form a ring.

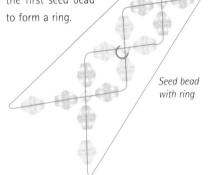

Seed bead with ring

2 Place the ring of beads in profile. Take the strand that is coming out towards you and thread it through two of the green bicones in the top and bottom flowers to form the brown flower on the first side. Leave this strand hanging after the last bead. Turn the ball around and repeat with the other strand.

Seen in profile

Jump ring

3 Thread one of the strands back through the seed bead at the centre of the top flower. Knot it 3 times and feed the ends through a few beads, avoiding the top seed bead.

4 **Dangle.** Using the pliers, form a ring at one end of a wire, for attaching the crystal teardrop (see p. 10). Finish the dangle and attach it to the ring of the flower ball.

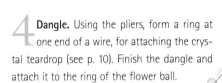

5 **Stringing the necklace.** Cut about 70 cm (28 ins) of 0.35 mm thread. Thread it through the bead at the top of the ball until the ball is in the middle, then follow the sketch. Place 8 bicones on each side, using the 3 colours in turn. Check whether the length suits you before finishing off the clasp.

Crimp bead

Crimp bead

Number of beads for the clasp to be adjusted

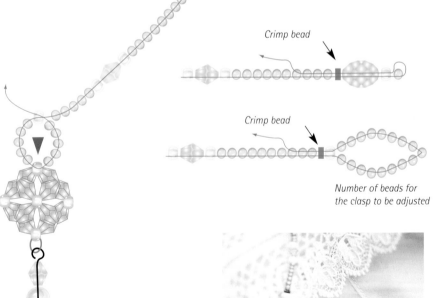

Materials

🔷🔷 Bracelet

4 mm bicones: 18 Light peach, 20 Light smoked topaz, 25 Chrysolite

White pearlised seed beads

Small beige pearlised seed beads

5 oval frosted glass beads in pink, about 1 cm long

Antiqued metal jump rings

Antiqued metal wire

Antiqued metal lobster-claw clasp

2 crimp beads

Nylon thread gauge 0.25 mm and 0.35 mm

Flat nose pliers and round nose pliers

Beading needles (recommended)

Bracelet

1 Make a flower ball – steps 1 to 3 of the necklace – placing the first beads as shown in the sketch.

2 Cut 70 cm (28 ins) of 0.25 mm thread. Make the first 2 interlacings of the second ball. On one of the strands, string 1 beige seed bead, 1 white seed bead, 1 peach bicone, 1 white seed bead and 1 beige seed bead, then pass the thread through the bicone at the centre of the top of the first ball. String 1 beige seed bead, 1 white seed bead, 1 peach bicone, 1 white seed bead and 1 beige seed bead. Pass the thread through the last seed bead of the un-finished ball. Thread the second strand through in the opposite direction. Complete the ball as before. Knot the ends and feed through.

Start of 2nd flower

3 Cut two 50 cm (20 ins) lengths of 0.35 mm thread. Slide them through the central white seed bead of the flowers at the ends of the motif, until the flowers are in the middle of the threads. Continue on each side by threading the strands through the beads as shown in the sketch (separately, together or crossing them depending on the motifs).

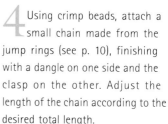

4 Using crimp beads, attach a small chain made from the jump rings (see p. 10), finishing with a dangle on one side and the clasp on the other. Adjust the length of the chain according to the desired total length.

Materials

  Earrings

4 mm bicones: 16 Light peach, 16 Light smoked topaz, 18 Chrysolite

White pearlised seed beads

Small beige pearlised seed beads

2 crystal teardrop beads in Light smoked topaz

2 fine-gauge antiqued metal jump rings

Antiqued metal French clips with shell motif

Nylon thread gauge 0.25 mm

Flat nose pliers

Beading needles (recommended)

N.B. Check that the holes in the white pearlised seed beads are big enough to take a ring plus two strands of 0.25 mm nylon thread.

Earrings

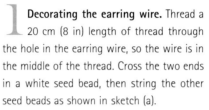

1 **Decorating the earring wire.** Thread a 20 cm (8 in) length of thread through the hole in the earring wire, so the wire is in the middle of the thread. Cross the two ends in a white seed bead, then string the other seed beads as shown in sketch (a).

Attach the top of the assembly above the shell by threading both strands back through the last bead (b).

Thread 1 green bicone onto both strands together, then cross them through the first seed bead. Knot the ends behind the shell and feed them back through a few beads. (c).

2 **Dangle.** Slip a jump ring into a white seed bead. Make a flower ball – steps 1 to 2 of the necklace (see p. 20) – reversing the order of the colours to place the pink flowers on the top and the green flowers on the back and front faces.

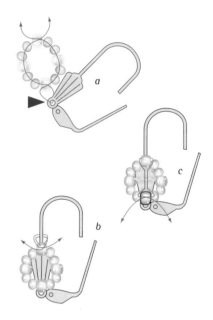

3 Cross the strands in the seed bead at the centre of the top flower. On one strand, string 4 beige seed beads, the earring wire, then 4 more beige seed beads, and pass the thread through the white seed bead of the ball. Thread the second strand through in the opposite direction. Knot 3 times. Attach the teardrop to the jump ring.

Beaded Scrolls

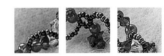

Bracelet

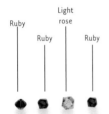

Ruby   Ruby   Light rose   Ruby

M a t e r i a l s

◆ Bracelet

28 size 4 mm bicones in Ruby

12 size 5 mm bicones in Light rose

1 size 6 mm bicone in Ruby for
the dangle

12 size 4 mm round beads in
coppery rose

Small copper-coloured seed beads

Nylon thread gauge 0.25 mm

Antiqued metal clasp

5 to 7 antiqued metal jump rings

Antiqued metal head pin

Wire cutters

Round nose pliers

Beading needle (optional)

1 Cut a thread 1.30 m (51 ins) long. String 10 seed beads in the middle of the thread and cross the strands in the last two. String 3 seed beads on one strand and 5 on the other, crossing the strands in the last 2 beads. Repeat the process to form a third ring.

2 On one strand string 1 round coppery rose bead, 1 Ruby bicone and 1 Light rose bicone, and on the other strand string 10 seed beads. Cross the strands in the last two seed beads. Start the whole motif again, reversing the strands and the direction of stringing.

3 For the next 8 alternating motifs, string 1 round bead, 2 Ruby bicones, 1 seed bead and a third Ruby bicone on one strand and feed the strand through the first bicone in the same direction. On the other strand, string 10 seed beads, then cross the strands in the last two beads.

Complete the bracelet with two of the motifs described in step 2, and with 3 rings of seed beads as explained in step 1. Knot the strands and feed through.

4 **Finishing.** On one side, attach a jump ring, then the clasp. On the other side, make a small chain with the remaining jump rings (see p. 10). Attach a dangle made with the 6 mm bicone (see p. 10).

Half bracelet, to be repeated symmetrically

Materials

Comb

18 size 4 mm bicones in Light rose

5 size 6 mm bicones in Ruby

Small copper-coloured seed beads

Nylon thread gauge 0.25 mm

Comb

Beading needle

Glue

Ring

6 size 4 mm bicones in Ruby

1 size 5 mm bicone in Light rose

Small copper-coloured seed beads

Nylon thread gauge 0.25 mm

Beading needle (optional)

Earrings

6 size 5 mm bicones in Light rose

18 size 4 mm bicones in Ruby

Small copper-coloured seed beads

Nylon thread gauge 0.25 mm

Antiqued metal French clips with shell motif

Beading needle (optional)

Comb

1 Cut 60 cm (24 ins) thread. String 7 small copper-coloured seed beads, 2 Light rose bicones, 1 seed bead and 1 Light rose bicone in the middle of the thread and go back through the first bicone. Add 1 seed bead and cross the strands by going back through the first 2 seed beads. Continue stringing as shown in the sketch for a length equivalent to that of the comb. Finish by knotting the ends and feeding them through.

2 Cut a thread of 50 cm (20 ins) and sew the motif to the comb, passing the thread through the Ruby and Light rose bicones on the rings of beads. Take care to cross the threads behind the comb. To finish off, knot the threads behind the comb and glue the knot before cutting off the ends.

Ring

Cut 50 cm (20 ins) of thread. String 10 seed beads in the middle of the thread. Cross the strands through the last two beads. String 3 seed beads on one strand and 5 on the other, and cross the strands in the last two beads. Make the central motif as shown in the sketch. Continue to the desired size by forming rings of 10 seed beads. Close the ring by using the beads from the first ring as part of the last one. Knot the strands, feed through a few beads and cut off.

Earrings

1 For each earring, cut 50 cm (20 ins) of thread. In the middle, string alternately 3 seed beads and 3 Light rose bicones. Cross the strands in the first seed bead.

2 On the left-hand thread, string 3 Ruby bicones, pass the thread back through the first seed bead then into the first Light rose bicone. Repeat the process twice as shown in the sketch and cross the thread again in the original seed bead.

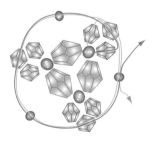

3 Form the small ball by crossing the two strands in the 3 outer Ruby bicones, inserting a seed bead in between each time. Finish by crossing the strands again in one of the outer seed beads.

4 **Finishing.** String 2 seed beads on each strand, then cross them in the ring of the earring wire. Thread the strands back in the opposite direction down to the base of the ring of beads. Knot the threads, feed through a few beads and cut off.

Imperial China

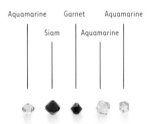

Aquamarine Garnet Aquamarine

Siam Aquamarine

Bracelet

Materials

Bracelet

41 sky blue 4 mm bicones (Aquamarine)

21 dark 4 mm red bicones (Garnet)

10 sky blue 5 mm bicones (Aquamarine)

10 bright red 5 mm bicones (Siam)

20 turquoise 6 mm oval beads

36 dark red 4 mm faceted beads (Garnet)

Red pearlised seed beads

Nylon thread gauge 0.25 mm

Beading needles (optional)

1 **Tile motifs.** Start by making the individual "tiles" that will later form the motifs for the bracelet, following the sketches. Cut 20 cm (8 ins) of thread per motif and make 5 tiles based on turquoise oval beads (sketches a and b) and 4 based on red faceted beads (sketches c and d). To finish, knot the thread and feed back through a few beads before cutting off.

a

c

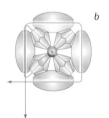

b

d

2 **Bar motifs.** Next make the two flow-ered "bars" to go at the ends of the bracelet. For each bar, cut 50 cm (20 ins) of thread. Make a base of 3 links with the red faceted beads and the seed beads (e), then make flower tiles with the blue 4 mm bicones (f). Knot the ends and feed through.

3 **Creating the bracelet.** Cut 2 threads 80 cm (32 ins) in length. In the middle of each, string 11 seed beads and make the loops for the clasp by threading the 2 strands of each loop through 1 more seed bead, 1 red or blue 4 mm bicone, then 1 more seed bead. Check that the size of the loops corresponds to the size of the beads for the clasp (5 mm bicones).
Then string 3 seed beads on each of the four threads and attach the first flowered bar by passing each thread through the seed beads and faceted beads of the bar as shown in the sketch (g).

4 Continue by positioning the tiles you have already made as shown in the sketch (i) by threading as shown in the sketch (h).

5 At the other end, pass the threads through the bar, then string 3 seed beads on each strand. Then on 2 strands to-gether string 3 more seed beads, 1 size 5 mm bicone – red or aquamarine – then 1 seed bead. Then pass the strands back in the op-posite direction through the bicone and the seed beads as far as the bar. Make sure there is no space between the beads and knot the threads. Feed through before cutting off.

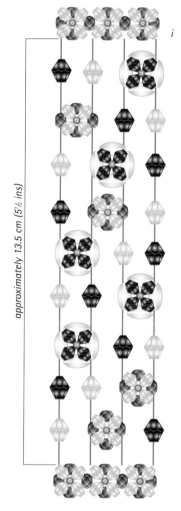

approximately 13.5 cm (5½ ins)

Use this sketch to set out the motifs. Adjust the number of beads in between to obtain the desired length.

Materials

Hairslide

4 sky blue 4 mm bicones (Aquamarine)

4 dark red 4 mm faceted beads (Garnet)

Red pearlised seed beads

Turquoise lacquered hairslide

Nylon thread gauge 0.25 mm

Glue

Earrings

8 sky blue 4 mm bicones (Aquamarine)

2 dark red 5 mm bicones (Garnet)

8 turquoise 6 mm oval beads

8 dark red 4 mm faceted beads (Garnet)

Red pearlised seed beads

Silver-coloured French clips with shell motif

Nylon thread gauge 0.25 mm

Beading needles (recommended)

Hairslide

Cut about 40 cm (16 ins) of thread. Make a flowered tile with the faceted beads and the blue bicones as shown in sketches (c) and (d) of step 1 of the bracelet. Cross the threads in one of the outer seed beads, then under the slide and again in the bead. Pass the threads through the faceted beads of the tile as far as the next seed bead.

Earrings

Attach the tile to the slide in the same way as on the other side. Knot the threads under the tile, cut off, and glue the knot.

1 For each earring, cut about 60 cm (24 ins) of thread. Make a flower tile with the faceted beads and the blue bicones as shown in sketch (c) of step 1 of the bracelet and the sketch below.

2 On each strand, string 1 oval bead. Then on both strands together, string 1 seed bead and 1 dark red 5 mm bicone.

Side view

3 Cross the strands in 2 beads, the ring of the earring wire and 2 beads. Feed back in the opposite direction through the bicone and the seed bead, string 1 oval bead on each strand and cross them in the opposite seed bead of the tile. Take one of the strands through all the seed beads and the faceted beads of the base. Knot the threads. Feed them back through a few beads and cut off.

Riviera

Bracelet

Blue
zircon
Aquamarine
Emerald

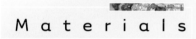

Materials

 Bracelet

4 mm bicones: 92 emerald, 33 turquoise
(Blue zircon)

149 pale blue 4 mm faceted beads

Green seed beads and 4 in blue

Small silver-coloured seed beads

Nylon thread gauge 0.25 mm

Silver-coloured jump rings: 1 of 3 mm
and 3 of 6 mm diameter

Silver-coloured lobster-claw clasp

Silver-coloured head pin

Wire cutters

Round nose pliers

Beading needles

*This bracelet is made up of 3 rows of
"links", with motifs following a
regular pattern.*

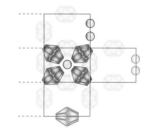

In the general sketch, the grid does not show the stringing, but it enables you to visualise the positioning of the beads and the emerald tile motifs.

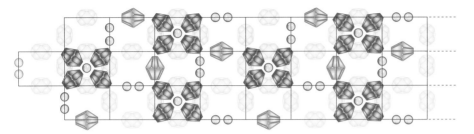

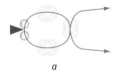

a

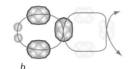

b

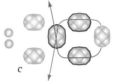

c

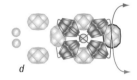

d

1 **Central row.** Cut 1.5 m (60 ins) of thread. String the beads for the clasp in the middle (a). Cross the strands in a faceted bead. Feed one of the strands back through the beads of the clasp, then string the beads for the next link (b).

2 **Emerald tile.** Feed the threads back in the opposite direction (c) and make the 1st tile (d).

3 Keeping the 4 motifs in the same order, (see general sketch), continue the central row link by link. Feed one of the strands back through the links containing bicones in order to strengthen them (e).
After the 8th emerald tile (the 7th, if the wrist is very slim), make the second loop of the clasp by feeding both strands into all the beads. Knot them, and set aside (f).

e

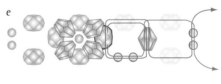

f

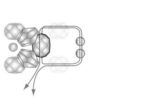

4 **Lateral Rows.** Still following the same procedure, make these one after the other, taking 1.5 m (60 ins) of thread for each (g). To make finishing off easier, start the 3rd row at the opposite end from the 2nd.

g

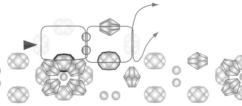

5 Complete each row by stringing the beads of the last link on a single strand, then knot the two ends (h). Feed all the ends back through a few beads, avoiding those at the edge of the bracelet.

h

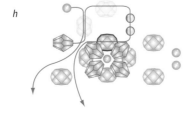

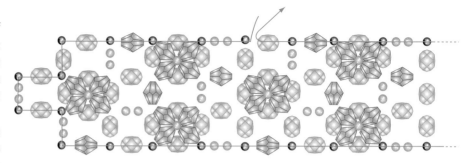

6 **Last round.** Take 60 cm (24 ins) of thread. Beginning in the middle of the bracelet, insert silver-coloured beads in the spaces between the links. When you have been all the way round, knot the strands and feed them through.

To make it even more perfect, you can take the thread once more through all the beads round the edge before finishing off. In this case, you will need 1.10 m (44 ins) of thread.

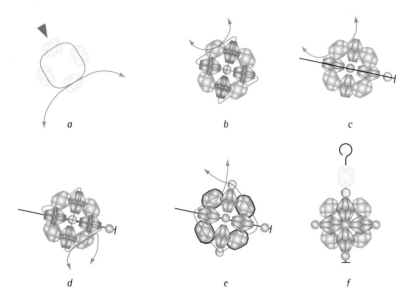

a

b

c

d

e

f

7 **Dangle.** Cut 25 cm (10 ins) of thread. String 4 faceted beads in the middle (a) and cross the strands in the last one. Make the tile for the first side (b).

Turn the work over. String 1 seed bead on a head pin. Place the pin on the piece you have just worked (c).

Make a second tile on the other side, holding the head pin firmly in the centre (d).

Pass the strands through the faceted beads so that you can add 2 more seed beads. Knot the ends and feed them back through a few beads before cutting off. (e).

String 1 seed bead and 1 faceted bead on the pin. Cut the pin off 1 cm (³/₈ in) above the beads and form the ring (f).

8 **Finishing off.** On one side, attach the clasp with a 6 mm jump ring. For the other side, join the remaining 3 rings together, with the smallest in the middle. Attach this little chain to the bracelet, then attach the dangle to the end of it.

If necessary, adjust the bracelet to the perfect size by altering the number of rings.

Earrings

Materials

Earrings

4 mm bicones: 4 emerald, 4 turquoise (Blue zircon)

8 pale blue 4 mm faceted beads

Green seed beads

Small silver-coloured seed beads

Nylon thread gauge 0.25 mm

Silver-coloured French clips with shell motif

Beading needle (optional)

1 Tile. For each earring, string 4 faceted beads in the middle of a 50 cm (20 ins) length of thread, then make a tile.

2 Small motif. Thread one of the strands back through the faceted beads, placing 1 green seed bead at each corner. Cross the second strand in the last seed bead. Then string 2 seed beads on each strand and cross them in a final seed bead.

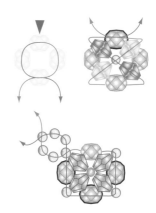

3 Slide the ring of the earring wire onto the back of the tile, pushing it in slightly. Attach the top of the small motif above the shell, by feeding each strand back through the last bead (a).

String 2 silver-coloured seed beads on both strands together, then cross the strands in the green seed bead at the base of the motif (b). Knot the strands behind the shell. Feed one of them back through the 3 beads at the bottom of the tile. Knot them again and feed the ends through before cutting off (c).

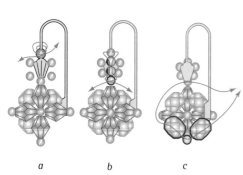

a   *b*   *c*

Back view

M a t e r i a l s

Long necklace

About 100 size 4 mm bicones in turquoise (Blue zircon), emerald and pale blue (Aquamarine)

About 65 pale blue 4 mm faceted beads

Green seed beads and 4 blue ones

Assorted blue, green and silver-coloured seed beads

Nylon thread gauge 0.25 mm

Beading needle

Ring

4 mm bicones: 8 pale blue (Aquamarine), 4 emerald, 4 turquoise (Blue zircon)

20 to 24 pale blue 4 mm faceted beads

Green seed beads

Small silver-coloured seed beads

Nylon thread gauge 0.25 mm

Beading needle (recommended)

Long necklace

The necklace shown measures 1.20 m (48 ins).

1 Make 10 tile balls, working exactly as for the dangle of the bracelet (explanation p. 10), but without inserting a head pin and using only one colour of bicones each time (add silver-coloured seed beads at stage e).

2 On a thread 1.40 m (56 ins) long, using a beading needle, string the tile balls and a mixture of seed beads, faceted beads and bicones. Space the balls out evenly according to whether you want the necklace to go round 1, 2 or 3 times. Knot the threads and feed them back through. You can also make a short necklace with a clasp.

Square ring with 4 tiles

2 Make the tiles for the right-hand column (c). Feed the threads back through as shown in the sketch, so you can make the tiles for the second column (d) and (e).

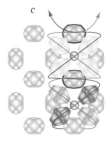

c

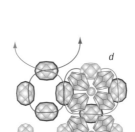

d

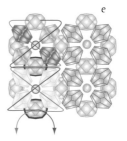

e

1 **Base.** First make a square base with faceted beads. Form the first "link" in the middle of a thread 1 m (39 ins) in length, then make the second by bringing the strands out at the side (a). Finish the base, leaving the strands at the bottom (b).

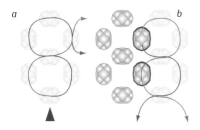

a

b

3 Going back through the faceted beads around the edge of the base, insert green seed beads in the spaces between. Cross the strands in the 3 beads in the middle of one of the sides (f).

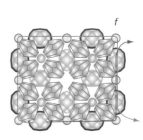

f

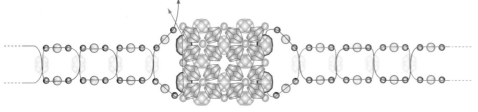

g
Number of beads to be adjusted to obtain the desired size.

4 **Ring.** String the beads as shown in sketch (g). Feed one of the strands through the 3 beads in the middle of the opposite side. Check the size. Knot the strands, then, if possible, feed them through all the beads in the ring before cutting off.

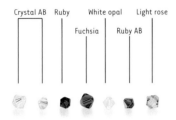

Crystal AB Ruby   White opal   Light rose

Fuchsia   Ruby AB

In the Pink

Earrings

Materials

🌸 Earrings

Small pale pink pearlised seed beads

12 diamond 5 mm bicones (Cristal AB)

10 white 4 mm bicones (White opal)

4 silver-coloured 2 mm round beads

Nylon thread gauge 0.25 mm

Silver-coloured French clips with shell motif

🌸🌸 Fuchsia ring

Small pale pink pearlised seed beads

5 pale pink 5 mm bicones (Light rose)

5 diamond 4 mm bicones (Crystal AB)

19 fuchsia 4 mm bicones (Ruby AB)

Nylon thread gauge 0.25 mm

🌸🌸 Pastel Ring

Small pale pink pearlised seed beads

5 diamond 5 mm bicones (Crystal AB)

24 diamond 4 mm bicones (Crystal AB)

Nylon thread gauge 0.25 mm

🌸🌸🌸 Comb (p. 42)

Small pale pink pearlised seed beads

25 diamond 5 mm bicones (Crystal AB)

10 white 4 mm bicones (White opal)

5 pale pink 4 mm bicones (Light rose)

5 diamond 4 mm bicones (Crystal AB)

5 fuchsia 4 mm bicones (Ruby AB)

Transparent comb

Nylon thread gauge 0.25 mm and glue

1 **Base of the motif.** Cut 60 cm (24 ins) thread. In the middle, string 5 diamond 5 mm bicones alternately with 5 seed beads. Cross the strands in the last seed bead, then pull them to form a pentagon. Next, string 1 small white bicone on both strands together, then string 5 pale pink seed beads on one strand. Feed the thread through the 1st seed bead again in the same direction and slide the ring of beads thus formed up against the small bicone. Thread the second strand through the last seed bead in the opposite direction.

2 **Centre of the motif.** Form the flower on the base by going back through the beads at the centre and the edge, adding a white 4mm bicone each time. Finish by stringing 4 seed beads on each strand.

3 Cross the strands in the ring of the earring wire. Thread them back in the opposite direction so they meet behind the motif. Knot, feed the ends through a few beads and cut off.

4 **Decorating the earring wire.** Cut another 50 cm (20 ins) thread. String a silver-coloured bead, cross the strands around the wire, then in the silver bead (a). String 4 seed beads on each strand and cross the strands in another silver bead (b), then behind the wire and again in the silver bead. String a 5 mm diamond bicone on both strands and cross them in the opposite silver bead. Knot discreetly at the back, then feed the end through a few beads and cut off.

a

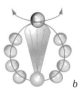
b

Rings

1 **Fuchsia ring.** Cut about 1 m (40 ins) of thread. To make the base of the motif, proceed as for step 1 of the earrings by stringing 5 pale pink 5mm bicones, 5 pale pink seed beads, 1 diamond 4mm bicone and 5 more pale pink seed beads.

2 Form the flower on the base by going back through the beads at the centre and the base, adding a 4 mm diamond bicone each time as shown in the sketch.

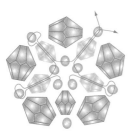

3 Make a circle round the motif with 4mm fuchsia bicones (a). On one strand string 1 bicone, 1 seed bead, 1 bicone and 5 seed beads. Pass the thread through the first 2 seed beads to form the centre of a motif. On the other strand, string 1 bicone and pass through 1 centre bead. String 1 bicone and pass through 1 seed bead at the top of the ring. Go back through the bicone in the other direction. Go back through 1 of the centre seed beads. On each strand, string 1 bicone and start another motif. Make 4 of these motifs. For the last motif (b), on one strand string 2 seed beads and go back through the seed bead of the circle's first motif. String 2 more seed beads and go through the very first one again to form the centre. Pass the other strand through 1 of the centre seed beads, string 1 bicone, go through the seed bead on top of the ring, go back through the bicone in the other direction and through the other centre seed beads to rejoin the other thread.

Both rings are made in the same way

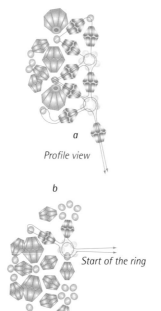

a

Profile view

b

Start of the ring

4 **Ring.** On both strands string 1 fuchsia bicone and seed beads to form a ring. When you have almost reached the right length, string 1 size 4 mm bicone and 1 seed bead, then on one strand only, string another bicone. Attach the ring to the motif by passing the thread through 1 seed bead, one fuchsia bicone and 1 seed bead. String a final 4 mm bicone and, after checking the length of the ring, knot the two strands. Feed the strands back through a few beads and cut off.

Bracelet

Bracelet

Small pale pink pearlised seed beads

1 fuchsia 6 mm bicone

25 fuchsia 5mm bicones (Ruby)

20 diamond 5 mm bicones (Crystal AB)

27 diamond 4 mm bicones (Crystal AB)

10 pale pink 4 mm bicones (Light rose)

10 fuchsia 4 mm bicones (Ruby AB)

Crimp bead

Nylon thread gauge 0.25 mm

Flat nose pliers

Beading needle recommended

1 **Loop for clasp.** Cut 1.20 m (48 ins) of thread. String about 15 pale pink seed beads in the middle, then 1 size 4 mm diamond bicone on both strands together. String another 3 seed beads and check whether you can pass a 6 mm bicone through the loop. Cross the strands in a 4th seed bead.

2 **Base of the motif.** On one strand, string 5 fuchsia 5mm bicones alternating with 4 seed beads. Go back through the last seed bead of the clasp, then pull the threads to form a pentagon. Then string a small diamond bicone on both strands, then 5 seed beads on a single strand. Pass the thread through the first seed bead again in the same direction, slide the ring of beads thus formed up against the small bicone. Feed the second strand through the last seed bead in the opposite direction.

3 **Centre of the motif.** Form the flower on the base by going back through the beads at the centre and the edge, adding a 4 mm diamond bicone each time as shown in the sketch.

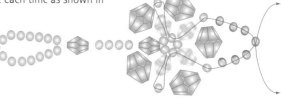

4 Then string 3 seed beads on each strand and cross in a 4th seed bead.

Make a chain of 9 motifs in the same way, alternating the colours – fuchsia and diamond – of the bases and centres (see photo) by repeating steps 2 to 4.

5 After the last motif, string 3 seed beads on each strand, then 3 more on both strands together. Finish by stringing a 4 mm diamond bicone, 5 seed beads, 1 crimp bead, the 6 mm bead and a final seed bead. Pass the strands back in the opposite direction through the bicone, the crimp bead and a few seed beads. Check the size of the bracelet. Make sure there is no movement between the beads and squeeze the crimp bead. Cut off the threads.

Comb

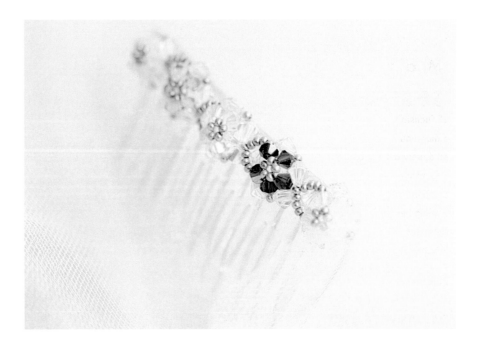

Cut 60 cm (24 ins) thread. Proceed as for the bracelet, this time forming a chain of 5 motifs (see steps 2, 3 and 4 of the bracelet). At the end of the last motif (finished in the same way as the one on the ring), feed one of the strands back through the beads of the base, make a knot, thread both strands through a few beads and cut off.

Then cut 40 cm (16 ins) of thread, pass it through a bicone at one end of the chain of motifs, and attach it to the comb by crossing the 2 strands at the back. Continue across the whole width of the comb. Finish by knotting the threads at the back of the comb on a level with the first tooth and add a spot of glue to fix the whole thing.

Hairslides

Cut about 40 cm (16 ins) of thread. Make the base, then the central flower (see steps 1 and 2 of the ring).

Next cross the threads under the slide, then pass them through the beads around the edge. Cross them again in the bicone opposite the seed bead attached to the slide. Cross the strands under the slide, pass them back towards the centre of the flower, then finally cross them under the slide. Knot and glue the knot under the slide.

Materials

Hairslides

Silver-coloured hairslide lacquered pink

Silver-coloured hairslide lacquered silver

Small pale pink pearlised seed beads

5 diamond 5 mm bicones (Crystal AB)

5 pale pink 5 mm bicones (Light rose)

5 fuchsia 4 mm bicones (Ruby)

5 diamond 4 mm bicones (Crystal AB)

Nylon thread gauge 0.25 mm

Materials

✿✿✿✿ Necklace

15 fuchsia 5 mm bicones (Ruby)

3 diamond 5 mm bicones (Crystal AB)

40 diamond 4 mm bicones (Crystal AB)

5 fuchsia 4 mm bicones (Ruby)

Small pale pink pearlised seed beads

2 crimp beads

Nylon thread gauge 0.25 mm

Silver-coloured head pin

9 silver-coloured jump ring 3 to 4 mm in diameter

Simple silver-coloured clasp

Flat nose pliers

Wire cutters

Beading needle

Necklace

1 **Central motif.** Cut 1.50 m (60 ins) of thread. Proceed as for steps 1 and 2 of the ring, adapting the colours (4 mm diamond bicones and 5 mm fuchsia bicones).

2 **Rose.** On one of the strands, string 2 diamond 4 mm bicones alternately with 2 seed beads, then 1 fuchsia 4 mm bicone, 1 seed bead and another diamond bicone. On the other strand, string 1 more 4 mm diamond bicone. Cross the strands in a seed bead. Then string 4 seed beads on one strand and form a ring by threading the strands back through as shown in the sketch.

3 Continue the rose in the same way, following the sketch.

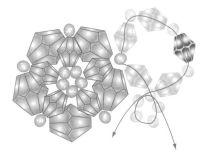 

4 **Symmetrical motifs.** Then form a new pentagon by stringing one seed bead on both strands, then 5 fuchsia bicones alternating with 4 seed beads on one of the strands. Feed the thread back through in the opposite direction.

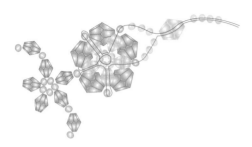

5 Next, string 1 small diamond bicone on both strands, then 5 seed beads on a single strand. Pass the thread through the 1st seed bead again in the same direction, slide the ring of beads formed up against the small bicone. Pass the second strand through the last bead in the opposite direction.

Put a flower on top, finishing with the petals opposite the hook. String 3 seed beads on each strand, then 1 size 5 mm diamond bicone on both strands. String 3 or 4 seed beads, and set aside.

6 To form the other part of the necklace, cut a thread 60 cm (24 ins) in length. Thread it through the centre of the rose flower, the 4 mm diamond bicone and the last seed bead. Form the pentagon surmounted by a flower as on the symmetrical motif.

7 **Finishing off.** Finish the necklace by stringing seed beads on both strands for about 15 cm (6 ins) on either side. Try the necklace on to check the length, string a crimp bead, a seed bead and a jump ring (see p. 10). Pass the threads back in the opposite direction through the seed bead, the crimp bead and a few more beads. Make sure there is no movement between the beads and squeeze the crimp bead. On one side, attach a clasp to the ring and on the other, make a small chain with 7 extra rings. Make a dangle (see p. 10) by mounting a 5 mm bicone on a head pin and attach it to the end of the chain.

You can adapt the necklace to form a pendant.

Frost Flower

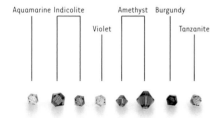

Materials

Mauve ring

4 mm bicones: 20 in Violet and 4 in Burgundy

4 iridescent light mauve 4 mm faceted beads

Short tubular seed beads in golden bronze

Nylon thread gauge 0.25 mm

Beading needles (optional)

Bronze ring

4 size 4 mm bicones in Burgundy

4 iridescent light mauve 4 mm faceted beads

Short tubular seed beads in golden bronze

Nylon thread gauge 0.25 mm

Beading needles (optional)

For all the jewels, begin by making the flower. The method is always the same, only the size and number of beads may change.

Mauve ring

1 Petals. Cut 80 cm (32 ins) of thread. In the middle, string 1 faceted bead, 3 bicones and 1 seed bead. Go back through the last bicone in the opposite direction. String 2 more bicones, then pass the thread through the faceted bead again in the same direction. String 1 seed bead before making the next petal. When the 4th petal has been completed, string a seed bead on the 2nd strand and feed this strand through the last faceted bead to close the flower.

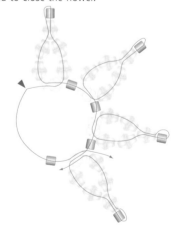

2 **Centre.** Form the centre of the flower with 4 Burgundy bicones and 1 seed bead, crossing the strands in the opposite faceted bead.

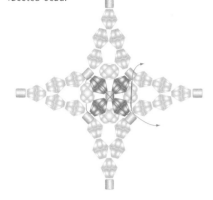

3 **Leaves and ring.** Make small leaves with seed beads using the same method as for the petals and form the ring, adjusting it to the size of your finger. Knot the ends in the middle of the ring and feed them back through a few beads before cutting off.

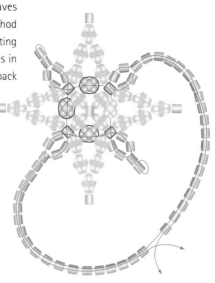

Bronze ring

1 **Petals.** Make the base of the flower, beginning with the seed bead petals, in the same way as for the previous ring. To do this, string 1 faceted bead, 7 seed beads, pass the thread back in the opposite direction through the last but one bead, string 5 seed beads and pass the thread through the faceted bead.

2 Next make the centre of the flower with the Burgundy bicones (see sketch for step 2 of the previous ring). Then form the ring, using the same method as for the mauve ring. The only change is in the number of seed beads for attaching the ring: 5 instead of 2 on each strand.

Materials

Blue hairslide

4 mm bicones: 12 in pale blue (Aquamarine) for the petals

4 size 5 mm bicones in smoked turquoise (Indicolite) for the centre

4 iridescent light mauve 4 mm faceted beads

Short tubular seed beads in golden bronze

Turquoise lacquered hairslide

Nylon thread gauge 0.25 mm

Purple hairslide

4 mm bicones: 20 in Burgundy for the petals

4 mm bicones: 4 in Violet for the centre

4 iridescent light mauve 4 mm faceted beads

Short tubular seed beads in golden bronze

Sky blue lacquered hairslide

Nylon thread gauge 0.25 mm

Hairslides

Make the flower of your choice as shown in the sketches for steps 1 and 2 of the mauve ring. Feed one of the strands back through the faceted beads and the seed beads at the base of the petals and finish by crossing the strands in a seed bead. Cross the strands under the slide, then above it through a different seed bead. Cross them again below, then above in a new seed bead, below and above in the seed bead at the base of the petals opposite the one you started from.

Knot the strands and cut off, after feeding them through a few beads.

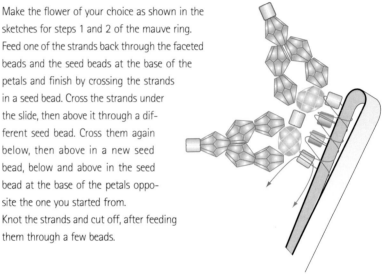

Pendant

Materials

Pendant

20 size 5 mm bicones in smoked turquoise (Indicolite)

4 size 4 mm bicones in Burgundy

4 iridescent light mauve 4 mm faceted beads

Short tubular seed beads in golden bronze

Fine gauge antiqued metal jump ring

Nylon thread gauge 0.25 mm and 0.35 mm

1 Flower. Cut 60 cm (24 ins) of 0.25 mm thread. Make a flower with smoked turquoise petals and a purple centre, following steps 1 and 2 of the mauve ring (see p. 46). Take one of the strands round through the faceted beads and seed beads at the base of the petals to meet the other strand. Knot the strands and leave. Turn the flower over so you can continue working on the back of it.

2 Leaves. Cut 60 cm (24 ins) of 0.35 mm thread. Thread it through a faceted bead, leaving an end of about 15 cm (6 ins). Using the longer end, start making the leaves with the tubular golden bronze seed beads, as shown in the sketch. Adjust the number of beads according to the size of bead used. With the other end of the thread, make the ring for the pendant in the same way.

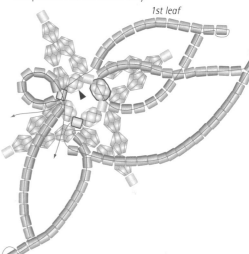

1st leaf

3 Finishing. Knot the threads of the leaves. Feed all the ends through a few beads and cut off. Fit the antiqued metal ring into the ring of beads.

Brooch

Materials

Brooch

28 size 5 mm bicones in violet (Tanzanite) for the petals

4 size 4 mm bicones in Burgundy for the centre

4 iridescent light mauve 4 mm faceted beads

Short tubular seed beads in golden bronze

Nylon thread gauge 0.25 mm and 0.35 mm

23 mm brooch back

1 **Flower.** Cut 60 cm (24 ins) of 0.25 mm thread. Make a flower with violet petals and a burgundy centre as in steps 1 and 2 of the mauve ring (see p. 46). This time use 7 size 5 mm Tanzanite bicones for each petal. Take one of the strands round through the faceted beads and seed beads at the base of the petals to meet the other strand. Knot the strands and leave.

2 **Leaves.** Cut 80 cm (32 ins) of 0.35 mm thread. Turn over the flower and make the leaves, passing the thread through the seed beads and a faceted bead at the base of the petals. Do not hesitate to alter the foliage according to the size of the beads.

3 **Finishing.** Knot the strands of the leaves together before fixing the jewel to the brooch back. Feed in the other ends.

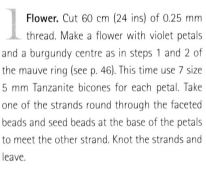

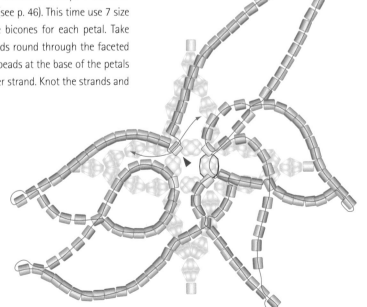

Rubies

Fuchsia   Siam   Cristal AB

Light Siam

Narrow ring with 3 tiles

Materials

🔷🔷 Narrow ring with 3 tiles

4 mm bicones: 4 Fuchsia, 4 dark red (Siam), 4 bright red (Light Siam)

2 silver-coloured 4 mm faceted beads

Diamanté seed beads

Small silver-coloured seed beads

Nylon thread gauge 0.25 mm

Beading needles

Square ring and narrow ring

1 In the middle of a thread 1 m (39 ins) long, string 1 faceted bead. Make a base of 3 links with diamanté seed beads, finishing with another faceted bead.

2 Make the 3 flowered tiles. Begin with the bright red flower and finish with the fuchsia flower, crossing the strands in the seed beads between the flowers. Use diamanté seed beads for the centres of the flowers.

3 Going back through the diamanté seed beads round the edge, insert silver seed beads on both sides. Cross the strands again in the right hand faceted bead and string the beads to form the ring. Close it by crossing the strands in the left hand seed bead. Check the size.

Number of beads to be adjusted according to the size of your finger.

4 Take each thread back through the first tile on the left (see sketch). String 1 silver seed bead on each strand, then on both sides of the ring, insert a new silver seed bead between each group of 2 beads. Finish with 1 silver seed bead on each strand. Pass 1 strand into the nearest tile (on the right in the sketch). Knot the ends under the base and feed them through a few beads before cutting off.

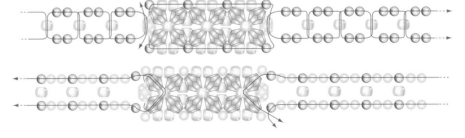

Square ring with 9 tiles

Materials

Square ring with 9 tiles

4 mm bicones: 4 Fuchsia, 8 dark red (Siam), 12 bright red (Light Siam), 4 iridescent diamond (Crystal AB)

38 to 42 silver-coloured 4 mm faceted beads

Diamanté seed beads

Small silver-coloured seed beads

Nylon thread gauge 0.25 mm

Beading needles

1 Base for the tile motif. Cut 1 m (40 ins) thread. Make the base for the tiles with faceted beads by stringing the first bead in the middle, then follow sketches (a) and (b).

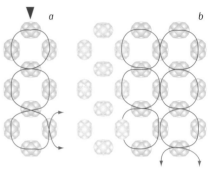

a   *b*

2 **Tiles.** Make these a column at a time as shown in sketches (c) to (g), going back through the faceted beads between the flowers and beginning with the bright red flower at the bottom right. Check carefully where the thread goes when you change column and use small silver seed beads for the centres of the flowers.

c

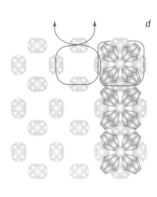

d   *e*

3 **Finishing the tile motif.** Going back through the faceted beads around the edge of the base, insert diamanté seed beads in the spaces (h). Knot the threads and feed back through a few beads, avoiding those where the ring will be attached.

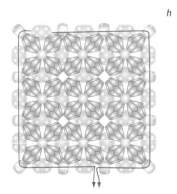

h

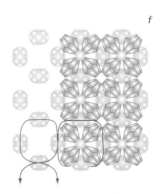

f   *g*

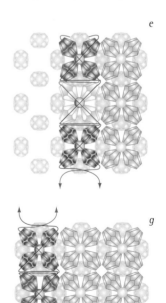

4 **Ring.** Feed another 60 cm (24 ins) of thread as far as the centre through the 3 beads in the middle of one side of the base (the right in the sketch). String the beads for the ring (diamanté seed beads and faceted beads). Close it by crossing the strands on the other side of the tile motif. Check the size.

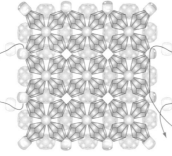

Changing the thread between the tiles and the ring avoids having to re-make the entire ring if the size is not right.

5 Going back through the beads at the edges of the ring, insert diamanté seed beads between the faceted beads. Feed one of the strands through the beads in the middle of the right-hand side of the tiles. Knot the ends and feed through a few beads before cutting off.

The ring made for the lozenge-shaped ring can be adapted for this ring.

Materials

Lozenge-shaped ring with 9 tiles

4 mm bicones: 4 Fuchsia, 20 dark red (Siam), 12 iridescent diamond (Crystal AB)

30 to 33 silver-coloured 4 mm faceted beads

Diamanté seed beads

Small silver-coloured seed beads

Nylon thread gauge 0.25 mm

Beading needles

Lozenge-shaped ring with 9 tiles

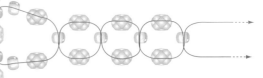

1 Make the base as for step 1 of the square ring. For the tiles, follow the instructions given in steps 2 and 3 of the same ring, but following the sketch on the right for the colours (the flowers around the edge are two-coloured).

Corner to which the ring will be attached

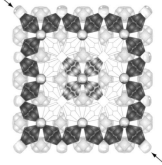

Corner to which the ring will be attached

2 **Ring.** Take another 60 cm (24 ins) of thread. Feed it as far as the middle through the 3 beads at one corner of the lozenge. String the beads for the ring. Close it by crossing the strands in the 3 beads at the opposite corner. Check the size.

3 Going back through the beads at the edge of the ring, insert silver beads in between the seed beads already strung. Feed one of the strands back through the beads of the first corner. Knot the threads, then feed back through a few beads before cutting off.

Number of beads to be adjusted according to the size of your finger.

Materials

 Pendant

4 mm bicones: 4 Fuchsia, 6 dark red (Siam), 5 bright red (Light Siam)

5 mm bicones: 2 Fuchsia

2 silver-coloured 4 mm faceted beads

Diamanté seed beads

Small silver-coloured seed beads

Nylon thread gauge 0.25 mm

Beading needles

Earrings

4 mm bicones: 16 Fuchsia, 16 dark red (Siam), 16 bright red (Light Siam)

2 silver-coloured 4 mm faceted beads

Diamanté seed beads

Small silver-coloured seed beads

Silver-coloured ear studs with ball and ring

Nylon thread gauge 0.25 mm

Beading needles

Pendant

1 Cut a thread 70 cm (28 ins) long. Make the base with diamanté seed beads, stringing the first faceted bead in the middle of the thread.

2 Make the tile motif, beginning with the bright red flower and going back through the seed beads between each flower.

3 Going back through the diamanté seed beads on both sides of the base, insert silver seed beads in the spaces in between. Then string the beads for the fringes on each strand.

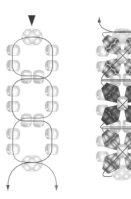

4 Go back in the opposite direction through the bicones and 3 of the silver seed beads. Cross the strands in the faceted bead. Pass the strands through the beads on both sides of the base. Cross them in the top faceted bead, then string the first beads of the clasp.

5 String the beads for the ring, crossing the threads. Feed them back through the bicone, then through the next seed beads on each side. Feed one of the strands through the faceted bead. Knot the ends and feed through a few beads, then cut off.

Adjust the size of the ring to the chain you wish to use to hang your pendant on.

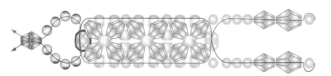

Earrings

1 For each earring cut 1 m (40 ins) of thread. Thread the ring of the earring wire to the middle and knot twice. Cross the strands in a faceted bead, then string a silver seed bead on each one (a).

Make two loose knots. Gradually tighten them, passing them over the stud behind the ball (b).

Pass the strands back through the silver seed beads, then cross them again in the faceted bead (c).

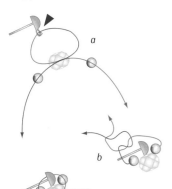

The end beads will slide into the loops of the butterflies.

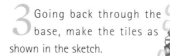

2 Make the base by forming 6 links using the diamanté seed beads. Finish it by crossing the strands in a seed bead, one loop of the butterfly and a final seed bead. Make sure you position the butterfly in the right direction in respect of the stud.

3 Going back through the base, make the tiles as shown in the sketch.

4 Going back through the diamanté seed beads along the edge of the base, insert silver seed beads in the spaces in between. Knot the ends and feed through a few beads before cutting them off.

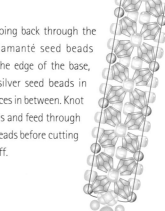

Edwardian

Pendant

Dorado

Crystal
metallic blue

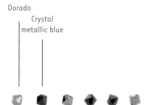

Materials

◆◆◆ Pendant

22 iridescent blue-green faceted beads

1 midnight blue 8 or 10 mm round faceted bead

4 mm bicones: 28 in Crystal metallic blue

Small gold-coloured seed beads

Nylon thread gauge 0.25 mm

Silky cord

Beading needles (optional)

1 **Base.** Cut 1.20 m (48 ins) of thread. Start by stringing 4 faceted beads alternating with seed beads. Form the 1st link by crossing the strands in a seed bead. Then on one of the strands (red), string 1 faceted bead and 1 seed bead, and on the other, string 1 faceted bead, 1 seed bead, another faceted bead, 1 seed bead and 1 faceted bead. Cross the strands in this last bead and continue the base, working in a clockwise direction, as shown in the sketch.

2 **Flowered tiles.** Still working clockwise, make a motif of flowered tiles with 24 bicones. It is sometimes difficult to pass the thread through some of the seed beads. In that case you have to "cheat" by passing under the previous threads. When you have finished the tile motif, feed one of the threads through the faceted bead on the short side of the central rectangle so you have a strand on each side of this bead.

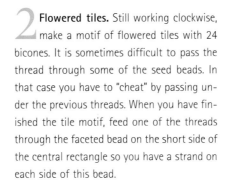

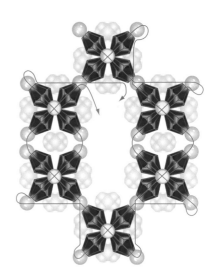

3 **Central motif.** On each strand, string 1 bicone, then on both strands together, 1 seed bead, the big round bead, 1 seed bead and then, on each strand separately, 1 bicone. Cross the strands in the faceted bead at the other side of the rectangle. Feed one of the strands through the nearest tile. Knot and set aside.

For the brooch and the choker, omit the top part that corresponds to the loop (as shown by the dotted lines).

4 **Seed bead lace edging.** Cut another 60 cm (24 ins) length of thread, feed it through the seed bead at the edge of the motif (marked start), and stop the end from slipping with a piece of adhesive tape. String 9 seed beads and pass the thread through the 2 seed beads in the middle of the side of the motif. Go back through the last bead in the opposite direction. Next, string 8 more seed beads, go through the next bead on the jewel and continue round the edge in the same way, stringing 8 seed beads each time. When you reach the top of the pendant, make the loop by stringing 12 seed beads and passing the thread back through the 4th seed bead. Thread 4 more seed beads to finish the top arch in the normal way. Finish the edging by forming the last arch with only 7 seed beads.

5 **Finishing.** When you have finished the lace edging of the pendant, make sure there are no spaces between the beads and knot the threads at the back of the jewel. Feed all the ends through a few beads. Thread the silky cord through the loop.

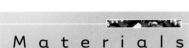

Materials

◆◆◆ Brooch

22 iridescent blue-green faceted beads

1 midnight blue 8 or 10 mm round faceted bead

4 mm bicones: 20 in Dorado

Small iridescent blue-green seed beads

Nylon thread gauge 0.25 mm

2.5 cm (1 in) brooch back

Beading needles (optional)

◆◆◆ Choker

22 gold-coloured faceted beads

1 gold-coloured 8 or 10 mm round faceted bead

4 mm bicones: 28 in Crystal metallic blue

Small gold-coloured seed beads

Nylon thread gauge 0.25 mm

Beading needles (optional)

Dark grey satin ribbon, 2.5 cm (1 in) wide

Dark grey thread and sewing needle

Make the choker as shown in the sketches for steps 1 to 4 of the pendant, but without forming the loop in step 4. When you have finished the lace edging of the pendant, make sure there are no spaces between the beads, knot the threads at the back of the jewel and feed them through a few beads. Then all you have to do is sew the jewel to the centre of the satin ribbon, positioning it so the motif is horizontal.

Brooch

Make the brooch as shown in the sketches for steps 1 to 4 of the pendant, but without forming the loop in step 4. To finish the brooch, make sure there are no spaces between the beads, knot the threads behind the jewel and position it so the motif is horizontal. Then pass the threads through the holes in the back of the brooch and fix it to the jewel, crossing the strands each time. Knot the ends, feed them through a few beads and cut off.

Choker

Earrings

1 **Base.** Cut 50 cm (20 ins) thread. In the middle, string 4 faceted beads alternating with 4 seed beads and cross the strands in the last faceted bead to form the base.

2 **Flower motif.** Then string 1 size 4 mm bicone on each strand, cross the strands in a seed bead, string 1 more bicone on each strand and cross the strands in the faceted bead on the opposite side.

3 **Finishing the motif and fixing.** Turn the work over and make the same motif on the other side. Then string 4 seed beads on each strand and bring the strands together by passing them through the 6 mm bicone. Then on one of the strands string 2 seed beads, the ring of the earring wire and 2 more seed beads, and feed the other strand through in the opposite direction. Knot the threads after making sure there are no spaces between the beads. Feed the ends through a few beads and cut off.

Make a second earring in the same way.

Rings

Materials

💎💎 Rings

16 gold-coloured or iridescent faceted beads

1 midnight blue or gold-coloured 8 or 10 mm round faceted bead

4 mm bicones: 16 in Crystal metallic blue

Small gold-coloured seed beads

Nylon thread gauge 0.25 mm

Beading needles (optional)

1 **Base.** Cut a thread 80 cm (32 ins) long. Start by stringing 4 faceted beads alternating with 4 seed beads in the middle of it. Cross the strands in the last seed bead. Then on one strand (red), string 1 faceted bead and on the other 3 faceted beads alternating with 3 seed beads. Cross the strands in the last seed bead. Continue the base as shown in the sketch.

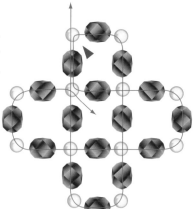

2 **Flowered tiles.** Make the flowers of the tile motif as for step 2 on p. 59, as shown in the sketch. Finish by passing one of the ends through the faceted bead in the central square, so you have one strand on each side of this bead.

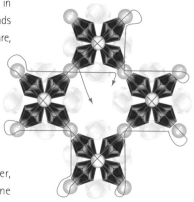

3 **Central motif and ring.** String 1 seed bead on both strands together, then the big round faceted bead and one more seed bead. Cross the strands in the faceted bead on the opposite side, then pass the strands through each of the 2 faceted beads and the next 2 seed beads on the nearest branch of the cross.

To start the ring, string 4 seed beads on each strand and cross the strands by going back through the last two. Start again by forming 8 or 9 links in the same way, until the ring is the right size for your finger. Close the ring at the side opposite to the start by passing each strand through the seed beads and faceted beads at the side of the cross. Knot the ends under the motif. Feed the ends through a few beads and cut off.

Red Fruits

Light Siam   Siam

Light Siam AB   Jonquil

Ball of bicones

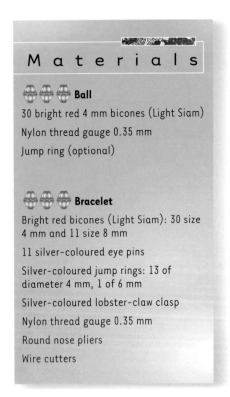

Materials

🔴🔴🔴 Ball

30 bright red 4 mm bicones (Light Siam)

Nylon thread gauge 0.35 mm

Jump ring (optional)

🔴🔴🔴 Bracelet

Bright red bicones (Light Siam): 30 size 4 mm and 11 size 8 mm

11 silver-coloured eye pins

Silver-coloured jump rings: 13 of diameter 4 mm, 1 of 6 mm

Silver-coloured lobster-claw clasp

Nylon thread gauge 0.35 mm

Round nose pliers

Wire cutters

This regular ball is made up of pentagons of interwoven beads. It can be worn alone as a pendant.

1 **Base.** Form a pentagon of 5 beads in the middle of 40 cm (16 ins) of thread.

2 **First row.** String 4 new beads for the first pentagon, crossing the strands in the last one, then pass the "inner" strand through the next bead on the base. On all sides of the base make 4 more pentagons, stringing 3 new beads for the second, third and fourth. For the final pentagon, string only 2 beads and pass the inner thread through the first bead of the first pentagon to form a row.

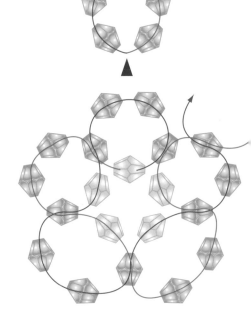

3 **Second row.** Proceed as for the first row, always threading the "inner" strand through the pentagons you have already made. String 3 new beads for the first pentagon, 2 for the next three, and one for the last. The ball gradually closes up.

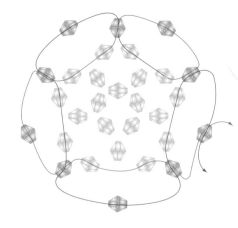

4 Finishing. Thread the strands through the top of the pentagons formed in the second row. Make 2 knots, one on top of the other. Feed the ends through a few beads before cutting off. To attach a ring, slide it on to one of the strands before knotting.

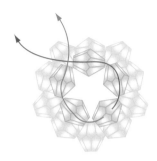

Bracelet

1 Make a ball with the 4 mm beads and add a small ring. Then thread each of the big bicones on to an eye pin. Cut the pin 1 cm (3⁄8 in) above the bead and use the pliers to form a ring.

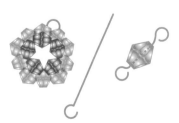

2 Use small jump rings to link 10 of these beads mounted on pins and then the clasp. Attach the last bead on a pin to the ring of the ball, then link this dangle to the bracelet with the three remaining jump rings.

To make the bracelet longer, try adding a few rings before the clasp.

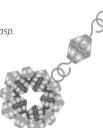

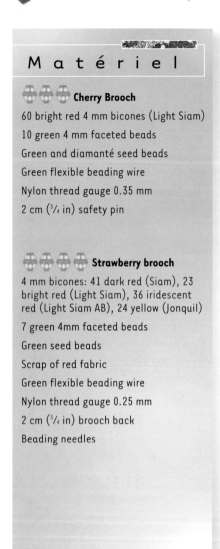

Cherry Brooch

1 Make 2 red balls as explained on the two previous pages (steps 1 to 4).

2 **Leaf.** Cut 30 cm (12 ins) of flexible beading wire. Bend it in half and make the leaf with faceted beads and green seed beads, as in the sketches. Close the leaf by wrapping the wire round twice between the first seed bead and the first faceted beads (c).

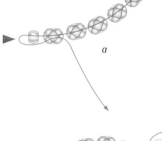

a

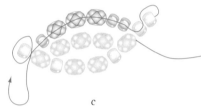

b

c

3 Turn the leaf over. Pass the right-hand wire through the ring of the safety pin, then "sew" it discreetly by passing the wire between the faceted beads. Twist the 2 strands of wire together, cut off leaving 0.5 cm (¼ in) ends and flatten these against the pin.

4 Cut 25 cm (10 ins) of flexible beading wire. Bend it in half and slip it into the ring of the safety pin. For the stalks, string diamanté seed beads on each strand. Fix each cherry by slipping the wire through the junction between 3 beads, then back into the stalk. Twist and cut the ends as for the leaf.

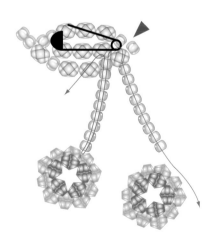

Strawberry brooch

Making the strawberry requires care, but the actual "weaving" is fairly simple. First you weave the two sides one after the other, superimposing them. The beads at the edge are shared, forming a kind of cornet that will be closed by a separate piece of weaving.

How to place the colours (identical for sides 1 and 2)

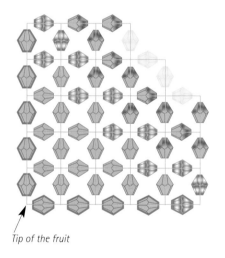

Tip of the fruit

Direction in which to weave the beads

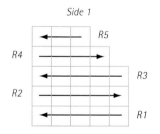

Side 1

R5
R4
R3
R2
R1

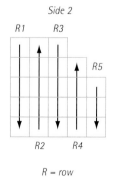

Side 2

R1   R3
R5
R2   R4

R = row

Jonquil   Light Siam

Light Siam AB   Siam

The beads outlined in blue are common to both sides.

1 **Side 1.** Cut about 2 m (7 ft) of nylon thread. Weave the first row by placing the first beads in the middle of the thread (a). Continue weaving, decreasing rows 4 and 5 as shown in sketches (b and c). The threads come out at the end of the last row.

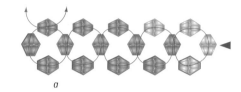

a

2 Side 2. Using the same threads, make the first "stitch" of the first row by stringing 3 beads on the upper strand. Cross the other strand through the last bead. For the following "stitches", always thread the left-hand strand through the bead at the edge of side 1. For the last "stitch" also go through the bottom bead.

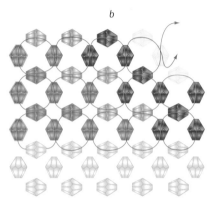

b

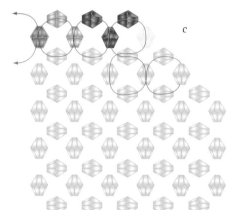

c

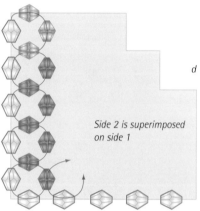

d

Side 2 is superimposed on side 1

3 Make the other rows as for side 1, going back through all the beads at the bottom of side 1 (e). Follow sketch (f) to see how to thread the strands when decreasing. At the end of the 5th row, the ends come out on the right.

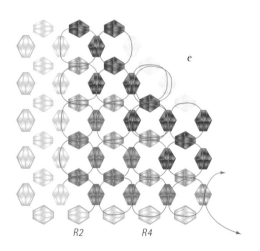

e

R2   R4

Note where the threads go when decreasing in rows 4 and 5.

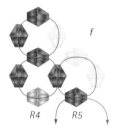

f

R4   R5

Detail of how to thread the strands when decreasing in rows 4 and 5.

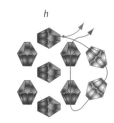

4 **To close.** Slightly open up the "cornet" that has been formed, position it with the opening towards you, with the threads pointing in the direction shown in sketch (c). Thread the lower strand back through the next bead on side 1. Start weaving as follows: 2 beads on the lower strand, cross. Thread the upper strand back through the next bead on side 2, string 2 new beads, cross.

Continue, going back through the beads on sides 1 and 2 and through the beads of the "stitches" previously made. When you are half way along, stuff the strawberry with fabric to give it bulk. To finish, tie 2 knots, pass one of the strands back through the 4 beads at the bottom, then feed both strands through a few beads before cutting off (h).

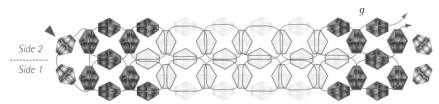

The beads outlined here in green are the new beads to be strung when closing the strawberry.

5 **The Leaves.** Cut 35 cm (14 ins) of flexible beading wire. String 1 faceted bead and 2 seed beads 15 cm (6 ins) from the end. Go back through in the other direction, except for the last seed bead. Make 6 similar fringes in the same way. Close by twisting the two strands 2 or 3 times.

6 Thread one of the strands back to the centre of this ring and make a new fringe to form the stalk. At the opposite end to where you closed the ring, make a loop between 2 leaves to which you can fix the stalk firmly, then twist the ends. Cut to about 5 mm.

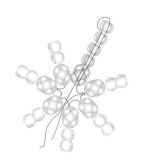

7 **Finishing off.** Stick the twisted ends of wire of the leaves into the strawberry. Leaving the end of a new length of nylon thread hanging, sew on the leaves. Stick the needle into the strawberry and pass it between the leaves around the central ring. Knot the 2 ends and feed them into the beads of the strawberry. Finally, firmly sew a brooch back onto the back.

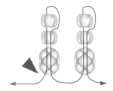

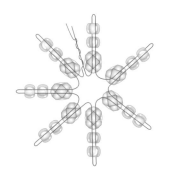

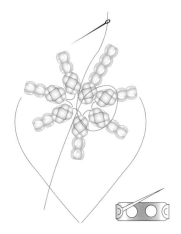

Garland of Flowers

Blue zircon   Blue zircon

Peridot   Jonquil

Ring

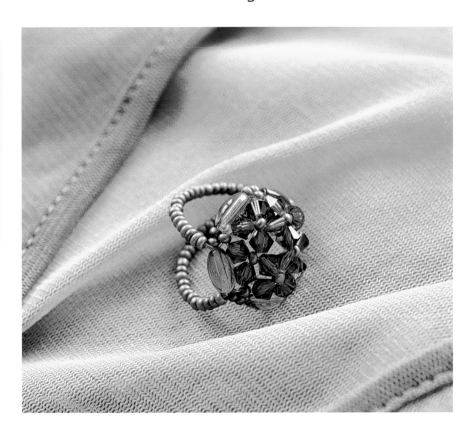

Materials

Ring

15 turquoise 4 mm bicones (Blue zircon)

5 anise green oval beads

Pearlised lime green seed beads

Nylon thread gauge 0.25 mm

Beading needles

Earrings

60 turquoise 4 mm bicones (Blue zircon)

10 sky blue 6 mm oval beads

Pearlised lime green seed beads

Gold-coloured French clips with shell motif

Nylon thread gauge 0.25 mm

Beading needles

1 **Motif.** Cut 90 cm (36 ins) of thread. String 3 bicones alternating with seed beads and cross the strands in the last bead (a). Next string 1 bicone, 1 seed bead, and a second bicone on 1 strand, and only 1 bicone and 1 seed bead on the other. Thread the first strand through this last seed bead and continue the motif as shown in chart (b).

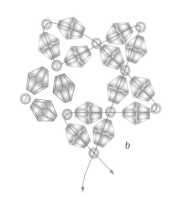

a

b

2 Edging for the motif. Add a round of oval beads by going back through the outer seed beads (red thread). Then, on the other strand, insert seed beads in groups of 2 (blue thread).

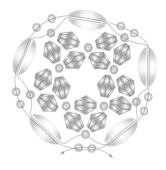

3 Ring and finishing. To make the ring, string seed beads on each strand. When it is long enough, pass the thread through the oval bead opposite the start of the ring and knot the ends. Feed the ends through a few beads and cut off.

Earrings

1 Ball: 1st half. Cut 90 cm (36 ins) of thread. Begin in the same way as for the ring, by making the motif (see charts for step 1 of the ring). Next make an edging of 5 oval beads, then a second round to insert the seed beads (just 1 each time).

3 Finishing. Next, string 2 seed beads on each strand and thread the strands through the earring wire. Then string 2 more seed beads on each strand and thread one of

the strands back through the nearest seed bead on the edging of the motif. Knot the ends, feed through a few beads and cut off.

step 1

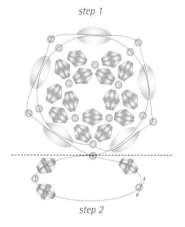

step 2

2 Ball: 2nd half. Then start the same motif again from the other side (see the lower part of the chart above), passing through the seed beads inserted on the 2nd round. Finish by crossing the strands in one of the seed beads of the edging.

Comb

1 Cut 90 cm (36 ins) of thread. In the middle, string 3 turquoise bicones alternating with 3 seed beads and cross the strands in the last seed bead. On one strand, string 1 green bicone (Peridot), 1 seed bead, and another green bicone, and on the other strand 1 green bicone and 1 seed bead. Cross the strands in the last seed bead. Continue the garland as shown in the chart (alternate the colours of the beads in groups of 3). When you have finished stringing, make a turn through the last motif to join the strands and knot them. Feed through and cut off.

2 Cut 50 cm (20 ins) of thread and attach the garland to the comb by threading the strands through the outer seed beads and crossing them several times behind the comb. Knot the ends and glue the knot to the back of the comb.

Graphic Stars

The bead colour key:

Montana	Topaz	Dorado	White opal blue	Ruby
Topaz	Black diamond	Jet hematite	White opal	

Materials

Pendant

6 size 8 mm and 14 size 4 mm bicones

Small seed beads

Nylon thread gauge 0.25 mm

Head pin

Round nose pliers and wire cutters

Beading needles

Advice:
Stretch the threads gently to avoid cutting them on the edges of the holes in the bicones.

Pendant

1 Centre of the pendant. Cut 1 m (40 ins) of thread. String 5 small bicones in the middle (a), then pass one of the strands back through all the beads (b).

2 Branches. On the right-hand thread, string 5 seed beads, 1 large bicone, then 4 seed beads. Pass the thread back through the 1st seed bead and then through the nearest bicone. Using this strand, make 2 more branches in the same way, then make 2 more using the left-hand thread. Cross the strands in the last small bicone.

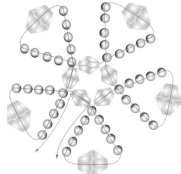

3 Pass each strand back through the 5 seed beads of the neighbouring branch, then cross them in a small bicone flanked by 2 seed beads.

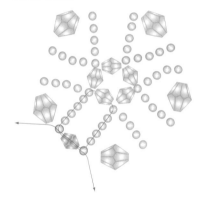

4 Edging of the pendant. With the right-hand thread, go back through the large bicones, adding small bicones flanked by 2 seed beads in between them. Bring the thread out after the last big bicone.

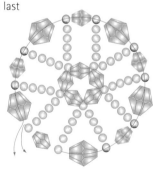

Instructions for the pendant continued on p. 76

5 **Finishing.** Make the dangle by stringing one large and one small bicone on a head pin (see p. 10). With the thread that was left over, start going round the pendant in the opposite direction. Come out after the 3rd large bicone.

For the loop, string 4 seed beads, 1 small bicone, and 13 seed beads, then go back through the bicone. String another 4 seed beads and go back through the small bicone flanked by 2 seed beads on the pendant. To strengthen the loop, go through the beads again (optional).

Continue round and come out after the large bicone opposite the ring. Make a loop in the same way, for attaching the dangle. Finish the round. Knot the 2 strands 3 times. Feed the ends through before cutting.

Tip
If the seed beads are too small to allow a number of threads to go through, modify the loop as shown in this sketch.

Brooch

Materials

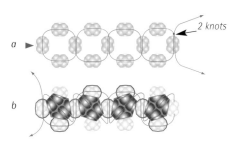

Brooch

6 size 8 mm and 4 size 6 mm bicones, in the predominant colour of your choice

14 size 4 mm bicones in a complementary colour or another shade of the same colour

13 faceted beads of the same colour as the small bicones

Small seed beads

Nylon thread gauge 0.25 mm

Head pin

2 cm (³⁄₄ in) brooch back

Round nose pliers and wire cutters

Beading needles

1 **Star.** Make this by following steps 1 to 4 of the pendant. Just change the shape of the loop when finishing, as shown in the sketch.

2 **Bar.** Cut 80 cm (32 ins) of thread, string the faceted beads as shown in sketch (a). Knot the threads. With the same threads, fix the 6 mm bicones in the centre of each link by going through certain of the faceted beads again (b).

3 On the upper strand, string seed beads, going back through the faceted beads of the surround. Do the same with the other strand until you reach the 3rd faceted bead of the bottom edge. Make a loop of seed beads for hanging the pendant, as shown in the sketch. Finish the round.

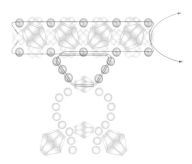

4 **Finishing.** Turn the work over, then sew on the brooch back, slipping the threads discreetly between the beads of the bar and crossing them. Knot and cut the threads.

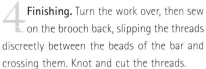

Necklace

Materials

Necklace

7 size 8 mm bicones in Black diamond

18 grey-blue 4 mm bicones (Montana)

Small silver-coloured seed beads

Nylon thread gauge 0.25 mm

2 silver-coloured head pins

Jump rings

Lobster claw clasp

2 crimp beads

Round nose pliers, flat nose pliers and wire cutters

Beading needles

1 Make steps 1 to 4 of the pendant, but bring the working thread of step 4 out after the last small bicone.

2 Make a dangle composed of 2 bicones and 2 seed beads on a head pin. Take the 2nd thread round the edge, remembering to make a loop for attaching the dangle. Make the chain to go round the neck by stringing seed beads and 2 small bicones on each strand as shown in the sketch. Make a second neck chain on a new thread.

3 **Finishing.** Finish on both sides using the 2 strands together. Add a second dangle.

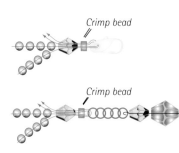

Crimp bead

Crimp bead

First published in Great Britain 2007 by Search Press Limited,
Wellwood, North Farm Road, Tunbridge Wells, Kent TN2 3DR

Originally published in France 2006 by Groupe Fleurus

Copyright © GROUPE FLEURUS, 2006
15/27, rue Moussorgski
75895 Paris Cedex 18

English translation by Cicero Translations

English translation copyright © Search Press Limited 2007

English edition edited and typeset by GreenGate Publishing Services, Tonbridge, Kent

ISBN-10: 1-84448-277-4
ISBN-13: 978-1-84448-277-1
N° L43729B

Index

First published in Great Britain 2005 by Search Press Limited,
Wellwood, North Farm Road, Tunbridge Wells, Kent TN2 3DR

Reprinted 2006, 2008

Originally published in France by Groupe Fleurus

© September 2004 GROUPE FLEURUS
15/27, rue Moussorgski
75895 Paris Cedex 18

English translation by Rae Walker for First Edition Translations Ltd, Cambridge, England

English translation © Search Press Limited 2005

ISBN 978 1 84448 106 4

Printed in China